Feel Strong Yoga

Contents

Written by Rachael Davis

Illustrated by Rea Zhai

Collins

What is yoga?

Yoga is 5,000 years old. It is made up of a set of poses that have cool names.

People that do yoga can be strong and fit.

We can all do yoga

big

little

old

You can do it your own way!

Note: If you feel pain when you do yoga, stop and get help.

What you need

✓ a yoga mat

See how they roll up!

✓ a **yoga block**

block

✓ room

This may be inside at home,

out in a field,

or on a boulder!

7

Sit and feel the air

Go slow!

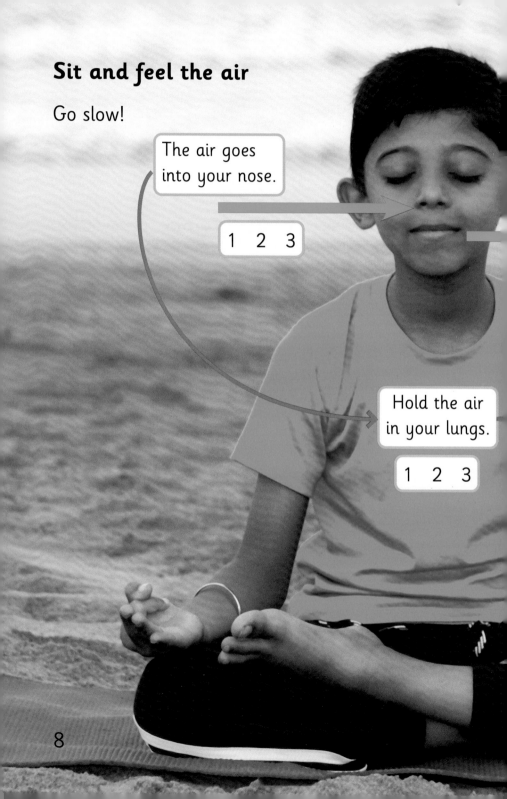

The air goes into your nose.

1 2 3

Hold the air in your lungs.

1 2 3

The tree pose

Lean the **sole** of your left foot on your right thigh.

Point your toes.

Reach up high with both arms and join your hands.

The chair pose

Stand and reach up high with both arms.

Pull your shoulder blades and elbows in tight.
Then bend down low like so.

The boat pose

Sit down and bend those legs.

14

Take both feet off the mat.
Push your legs and arms out.

Lean on your
"**sit bones**".

The cobra pose

Rest on the mat. Tuck your arms in, with your hands by your shoulders.

Then push your **torso** up like so.

Mat poses

Start like so.

Down dog pose

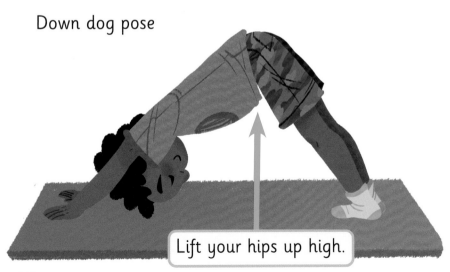

Lift your hips up high.

Cow pose

Tilt your spine.

Look up.

Cat pose

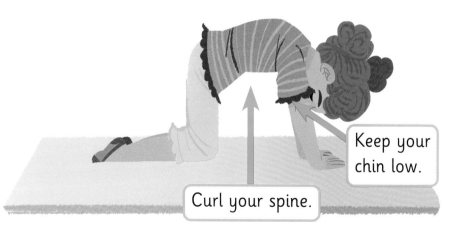

Keep your chin low.

Curl your spine.

Poses with a yoga block

The name of this pose is a shape. Can you see the shape?

21

What is flow yoga?

In flow yoga you go from pose to pose with a slow **inhale** and **exhale**.

Note: **Vinyasa** is the name of a set of yoga poses.

What makes yoga good?

Yoga shows you how strong you can be.

It helps you to bend ...

and feel **tranquil**.

Yoga is good for the mind.

25

Make time for yoga

You will get better each week.

Yoga makes you fit and strong. This can help you to be better at different sports.

Glossary

exhale to let go of air from the lungs and nose

inhale to take air into the nose and lungs

sit bones a yoga term for the bones that support you when you sit

sole the part underneath a foot

torso waist, chest and shoulders

tranquil a clear and still state of mind

vinyasa a set of yoga poses in flow yoga

yoga block a brick to help you bend into a yoga pose

Index

How to be a yoga expert

Make time and find room.

Take a seat and feel the air.

Do yoga poses.

Feel strong!

 After reading

Letters and Sounds: Phase 5

Word count: 380

Focus phonemes: /ai/ ay, a-e, ey /ee/ ie, ea /igh/ i-e, i /oa/ o, oe, ow, oul, o-e

Common exception words: of, to, the, into, by, pull, push, we, be, have, do, little, when, what, people, all, your, out, you

Curriculum links: Physical education

National Curriculum learning objectives: Reading/word reading: apply phonic knowledge and skills as the route to decode words; read accurately by blending sounds in unfamiliar words containing GPCs that have been taught; Reading/comprehension (KS2): understand what they read, in books they can read independently, by checking that the text makes sense to them, discussing their understanding and explaining the meaning of words in context; identifying main ideas drawn from more than one paragraph and summarising these, identifying how language, structure, and presentation contribute to meaning

Developing fluency

- Demonstrate reading the instructions on pages 10 to 11 with a tone of gentle authority.
- Take turns to read a page. Check that your child notices the question marks and reads them with a questioning tone.

Phonic practice

- Focus on the spellings of /oa/ sounds. Ask your child to read the following words and point to the letters that make the /oa/ sound:
  go   shoulder   nose   pose   yoga   boulder   low
- Repeat with the following and ask your child to spot the word that does not contain the /oa/ sound. (*down*)
  elbow   low   down   flow   slow

Extending vocabulary

- Reread pages 14 and 15. Turn to pages 20 and 21 and ask your child to make up similar instruction sentences to go with the picture.

  Encourage your child to begin each sentence with a verb and include names for parts of the body. (e.g. *Stand with your feet apart*; *Put one hand flat on the block*; etc.) Repeat for the three positions on page 26.